Celebrating the Offering

Melvin Amerson
and
James Amerson

DISCIPLESHIP RESOURCES

P O BOX 340003 • NASHVILLE, TN 37203-0003
www.discipleshipresources.org

Cover design by Thelma Whitworth.

ISBN 13: 978-0-88177-526-6

Library of Congress Cataloging-in-Publication Data on File.

COMMENDATIONS

"*Celebrating the Offering* is an exciting biblically based invitation to appreciate the liturgical richness of the offering as a major part of worship. Too often the church has viewed the offering as a necessary evil, needful only for the fiscal support of the church and denominational programs. Celebrating the Offering invites us to see the spiritual value both in the process of and the participation in worship through sharing and giving. Offerings are unto the Lord and in response to the Lord's presence and power. Thanks to Melvin and James Amerson, the church can be freed to celebrate the offering."

—*Dr. Michael R. Battle, The Interdenominational Theological Center, Atlanta, Georgia*

"*Celebrating the Offering* is an absolute must read for anyone serious about nurturing generosity in the congregation. Don't stop after reading this book. Get a copy for everyone on your stewardship and worship planning teams and together read, mark and actively explore how these invaluable suggestions can be put into practice for enhancing year-round stewardship education."

—*Tom Gossen, Executive Director, The Episcopal Network for Stewardship, Wichita, Kansas*

"As a consultant to the 630 or so ELCA congregations in Ohio, I'm very much aware that, as the Amerson brothers indicate, the offering is more often regarded as a necessary evil rather than an opportunity for worship. I believe this work will go a long way in helping our members raise their awareness of the offering as a high point in worship rather than an interlude."

—*Eugene Grimm, Stewardship Specialist for the Evangelical Lutheran Church in America*

"It is a real pleasure to know and work with brothers Melvin and James. The two are committed to their calling, the church and developing faithful disciples of Jesus. I am delighted they have offered us this book. *Celebrating the Offering* is a theologically insightful look into the creation of a generous culture and spirit within congregations. I commend it to your reading."

—*Tom Locke, President, Texas Methodist Foundation*

"We are blessed to have the Amersons contribute to our sense of celebration by including the time of offertory, as we share our tithes, gifts, and sacrificial offerings in the context of worship. Unlike the Zebedee boys who sought place and position without regard for their colleagues, we are encouraged by the Amerson brothers who give primacy and priority to this celebratory act in our spiritual worship by advancing the emotional health of the household of faith. Fantastic!"

—*Dr. Frank Portee, III, Pastor/Chief Spiritual Officer, Church of the Good Shepherd United Methodist Church, Willingboro, New Jersey*

CONTENTS

ACKNOWLEDGEMENTS

From start to finish the Lord's hand was on this stewardship resource. Writing a book is always a process. In this project, there were a number of individuals who made a variety of contributions. Some gave words of encouragement, others prayers, a few input and critique. All of those contributions were needed for this project to come to fruition.

A personal highlight of writing this book was the opportunity of co-authoring Celebrating the Offering, with my brother, friend and colleague.

I would like to acknowledge:

A special thanks to my parents, Tommy and Loretta Amerson, who provided many words of encouragement for my brother and me throughout each stage of this book;

Michele, my family, friends, and colleagues who supported this project with prayers, and those who submitted written prayers and litanies;

Patti Simmons who graciously edited the manuscript in its formative stage;

The Texas Methodist Foundation for allowing me the privilege of being in ministry with pastors, laity, congregations, and annual conferences across the state of Texas.

George Donigian, my editor, and contributor of the chapter ending prayers and litanies.

Special acknowledgements to:

The late Reverend LaValle Lowe, Jr., my childhood pastor who helped develop a generation of faithful givers at St. Paul United Methodist Church in San Antonio, Texas;

Lastly, to the late, Dr. Mance C. Jackson, Jr., who taught church administration at the Interdenominational Theological Center, and regularly shared his testimony of God's generosity in his lectures.

Melvin Amerson

No person gets where they are in life without the encouragement of others. I am indebted to the men and women, youth and children who have supported my ministry over the years. Thanks to those who shared countless conversations with me on stewardship—I appreciate your wisdom, experience and insight. Also, a special thank you to those who have struggled with me on the theme of stewardship and offerings in the church and stirred my interest in knowing that it is important to celebrate God with all that we have.

God has blessed me with wonderful examples of stewardship and generosity at several churches where I have served, including: Ernest T. Dixon United Methodist Church, San Antonio, TX, St. John's United Methodist Church, Corpus Christi, TX, and Hoosier Memorial United Methodist Church, Atlanta, GA.

A special thanks to the persons who have taught me to be generous because of their kind backing, my parents, Tommy and Loretta Amerson, friends Sandra Cranford, Chris Davis Garcia, and to others who contributed acts of worship, litanies, and prayers for this project.

To Simpson United Methodist Church, Austin, TX, who holds me accountable to the importance of good stewardship in the ministry context, thank you for the way you uphold me.

To my closest and dearest colleague and friend, Melvin. I have learned an important spiritual discipline through you. It has been a blessing to have partnered with you on Celebrating the Offering.

James Amerson

FOREWORD

When the topic of the offering is mentioned in the church, many persons are immediately turned off by the conversation. Spirituality should not be sullied by money, so the argument goes. In both Old and New Testament scriptures, however, the meaning and significance of the offering is astonishingly clear and Godly. God gives abundantly and generously. So also the people of God are meant to share their gifts joyfully and generously.

Celebrating the Offering reminds and instructs us to honor our heritage as a community of faith. As brothers in ministry, Melvin Amerson and James Amerson bring years of tested experience in this area of worship. Their insights and practice convey a deep understanding of this often misunderstood and maligned component of our lives as followers of Christ: simply put, our faith informs the way we live, including how we spend our money.

I appreciate the passion that they bring to *Celebrating the Offering*. They offer to the people of God an act of generosity and courage to be lived out daily. Their treatment of the offering is biblical, theological, practical and helpful so helpful, in fact, that *Celebrating the Offering* should be read by both clergy and laity. Understanding the history and theology of the offering, and incorporating the book?s practical ideas into congregational life will encourage and enthuse the pulpit and pews with an ever-increasing joy in the Lord.

Celebrating the Offering brings our faith closer and closer to the center of our lives, both personally and corporately. The offering becomes an act of worship that is a natural expression of—not just what we do with our gifts—but who we are as Christians. *Celebrating the Offering* will be a pay-off to the church.

Dr. Zan W. Holmes, Jr.
Pastor Emeritus St. Luke "Community"
United Methodist Church
Dallas, Texas

INTRODUCTION

Let's celebrate the offering! The offering is part of the worship experience. However, too often the offering appears to be a segment of the service that is disengaged from the rest of the service. There are many reasons for the impression that the offering is the odd-lot in the order of worship. Planning the offering is essential in making it an integral part of worship, as we praise God from whom all blessings flow.

In many congregations the offering just happens without much forethought. The offering is not only a time to worship the Lord through the presentation of believers' tithes and offerings, but it is also a time to recognize how blessed we are. Through planning and education, worshippers will begin to feel and see the offering as a time of celebration.

Believers and followers in both the Old and New Testaments presented tithes and offerings as an offering unto the Lord. The presentation of tithes and offerings was an act of worship. Today, the offering is viewed differently due to influences outside of the church, but perhaps most specifically because of the influence of consumerism in our culture. Many people seem to think that they need "pay" only what they perceive as the worth of the service. Such thinking goes against biblical tradition and church history. If we are honest, we know this perception influences many people. In essence, the offertory has in part been disconnected from worship. Across many denominations churches have witnessed decades of declines in percentage giving, while incomes have increased significantly. Society for the past few generations has considered money and material possessions to be non-spiritual, so giving has become a topic that pastors and laity shy away from, even though it is an act of worship. To address this problem, pastors and worship leaders must become more intentional in reconnecting the offering as a part of the worship experience.

As siblings and as brothers in ministry, we want to share ideas on planning the offering and creating an atmosphere of worship and celebration during the offering. This book is designed for pastors, worship leaders, and worship committees who desire not only to reconnect the offering with the rest of the worship service, but also to add excitement and enthusiasm to the act of giving.

Below is a brief summary of the chapters in Celebrating the Offering:

- Chapter one covers the historical development of the offering in the Old Testament as an act of worship. We will share biblical stories that show the importance of celebrating the offering in the Old Testament;

- Chapter two will cover practices of giving in the New Testament;

- Chapter three gives ideas and plans on how to set the tone or mood for the offertory;

- Chapter four shares several tips and ideas on how to enhance worship through giving;

- Chapter five discusses the role of clergy in celebrating the offering;

- Chapters six discusses the role of laity in celebrating the offering;

- Chapter seven provides suggestions on involving children and youth in worshipping through giving.

Celebrating the Offering was written to provide churches large and small with a resource that will help reconnect the offering as an act of worship.

Pastors and worship leaders can use this book as means of revitalizing the spirit of generosity in their congregations. Deuteronomy 16:15, says, " . . . and you shall surely celebrate." Let's celebrate!

CHAPTER ONE

The Offering in the Old Testament

"They shall not appear before the Lord empty-handed; all shall give as they are able, according to the blessing of the Lord your God that he has given you."

DEUTERONOMY 16:16C-17

From the beginning of recorded biblical history, offerings have been presented to God our creator. Even before the Law of Moses, there were established guidelines and expectations for people who gave offerings. Throughout the Old Testament a variety of offerings and sacrificial offerings were given in addition to the tithe. Offerings were presented to honor God. Even though people lived under the Law in the

Old Testament, the Law ordered the lives of people in a grace-filled manner. More importantly, the offering was a means of worshipping God.

The word offering has two broad meanings. An offering is the general act of giving, usually in addition to the tithe; it is also the rendering of a particular type of gift in response to a specific act or ritual. Sacrificial offerings were the presentation of animals or fat portions of animals burned at the altar and consumed by God. Offerings fell into three broad categories: gifts and tributes, alimentary and expiatory. Gifts and tributes were given to honor God and find favor. These are some of the offerings and the reasons members of the community gave gifts and tributes: propitiatory (find favor or appeasement), tributary (first fruits and tithes), votive (voluntary vow), thanksgiving (acknowledged favor), and freewill (impulse gift). These offerings were given to honor God and find favor. [See *The Interpreter's Dictionary of the Bible* (Nashville: Abingdon Press, 1962) article on *Sacrifice*, pp. 147-159.]

Alimentary offerings were offerings that were presented on a regular or scheduled basis. Some of these offerings took place daily. The others took place throughout the duration of the festivals.

The expiator offering's focus was on repentance. The sin offering falls within this class of offerings. An offering was giving for repentance by the person who committed a sin knowingly or unknowingly. The guilt offering is often confused with the sin offering. The origin offering implies wrongdoing, but some biblical scholars believe the offense fell within the area of civil law. These offerings were more like restitution or fines than an offering. Still, with the variation of offerings, they were a way to honor God or a means of atonement.

Honoring God with offerings has been with us since Cain and Abel, the sons of Adam and Eve. The Cain and Abel story centers on their offerings to God. Cain is a farmer and tiller of the ground, while his brother Abel is a keeper of animals. They both present God with an offering. Cain gives an offering of fruit from the ground. His brother Abel offers the fat portions of firstlings from his flock. God looked more favorably upon Abel's offering than Cain's. There are many theories concerning why God favored Abel's offering over Cain, but most feel Abel gave the best he had to offer, so God favored his offering as opposed to his brother's. While we most frequently remember the story of Cain and Abel for the murder that happened, we need to first think of this as the first biblical record of an offering presented to God.

It was God who commanded Noah to build an ark, for his family and himself, along with a pair of every living animal prior to a great flood that was the result of rain for forty days and forty nights. God caused the flood in order to eradicate violence and corruption on earth, but God spared Noah's family because he was found righteous. Noah was the first to construct an altar for offerings to God. After the waters from the flood receded, he built an altar to the Lord, prepared very clean animals and birds, and placed the offering to burn on the altar. The fragrance from the burnt offering pleased God.

In Genesis 28, Jacob the son of Isaac left home after deceitfully acquiring his brother Esau's inheritance. On his way towards Haran, he settled down for the evening in a place, where he took a stone to sleep on. That night Jacob had a dream of a ladder that extended to heaven, with angels of God ascending and descending from earth to heaven. God spoke to Jacob and told him that God would bless him and his offspring, and God would be with him. When Jacob rose the next morning, he took the stone he had slept on and set it up as a pillar. He poured oil on top of it and called it Bethel, which means "The House of God." There, Jacob declared the pillar a house of God and vowed to tithe. For Jacob giving became an act of worship.

Still later in the Pentateuch, after Pharaoh released the Israelites, Moses and his people began to wander in the wilderness. Soon, they grew restless and complained to Moses about the lack of direction and provisions, and desired to return to Egypt. God spoke to Moses and instructed him to give the people strict instructions if they wanted to be blessed with provisions. God then covered the ground with manna for them. Later in Exodus 17, Amalek fought the Israelites at Rephidim and Moses asked Joshua to gather men to fight Amalek. God guided them through the battle and Joshua defeated Amalek. Jethro, Moses' father-in-law, was in awe of God's power. In fact, he was so excited to hear of Moses' story of how God blessed and delivered the Israelites from Pharaoh that he gave a burnt offering and sacrifices to God. For Jethro, an offering was the proper way to celebrate and honor God for wondrous acts (Exodus 18:10-12).

"No one shall appear before me empty handed," is found in Exodus 23:15, 34:20. In these passages God declares that believers must honor God by presenting an offering when they come into Lord's presence, particularly at the three annual festivals, the Feast of Unleavened Bread, the Feast of Weeks, and the Feast of Tabernacles. Moses says, "They shall not appear before the Lord empty handed, all shall give as they are able, according to the blessing of the Lord your God that he has given you" (Deuteronomy 16:16-17). This further indicates that giving is an act of worship and a sign of faithful commitment by the people of God.

Consider also King David as he spoke to Araunah

in 2 Samuel 24:24-25. David says "I will not offer burnt offerings to the Lord my God that cost me nothing . . . " Giving is not only an act of worship. Here, giving is a sacrifice that is more than a tip or a token amount. When honoring and worshipping God, our gift must be of value and a representation of our love for God. Accordingly, Proverbs 3:9 provides instructions for believers to "Honor the Lord with your substance and with the first fruits of all your produce." The psalmist tells us in Psalms 96:8, "Ascribe to the Lord the glory due his name; bring an offering, and come into his courts.

In Malachi 3, God showed anger and disappointment when the people failed to honor God with their tithes and offerings. Further, these acts of omission indicate they were giving their tithes and offerings elsewhere. This prompted God to challenge the people to "Bring the full tithe into the storehouse." God not only posed a challenge, but also promised to shower the people with blessings if they worshiped through giving in God's house.

The Old Testament contains a wealth of biblical stories, laws, mandates, and traditions, which give rise to a foundation for the presentation of tithes and offerings. During Old Testament times, believers lived under the "Law" that set the spiritual framework for the New Testament. Cain and Abel enact the first presentation of on offering in the Bible, Noah constructs the first altar, God shares expectations regarding giving in Exodus 23:15, and lastly, God provides instructions concerning where we should present our tithes and offerings in the third chapter of Malachi.

We tend to think of Old Testament people as those who live in covenant relationship with God. Sometimes we fail to notice that the people give in response to God. Their gifts are signs of their love and faithfulness. Some gifts, such as burnt offerings, seem extravagant because we do not burn our gifts and often we expect accountability for these gifts. Other gifts and offerings in the Old Testament supported widows and orphans and aliens, something our tithes and offerings do today. When you read Old Testament stories, notice the giving that takes place and join in the spirit of faithfulness and generosity.

In the spirit of Old Testament givers, join in this litany of thanks:

L: I will give thanks to the Lord with my whole heart;

P: **We will tell of all your wonderful deeds.**

L: I will be glad and exult in you;

P: **We will sing praise to your name, O Most High!**

(Based on Psalm 9:1-2)

CHAPTER TWO

The Offering in the New Testament

"Each of you must give as you have made up your mind, not reluctantly or under compulsion; for God loves a cheerful giver."

2 CORINTHIANS 9:7

The offering in the New Testament developed a different focus. Believers were no longer bound by the legalistic interpretation of the "Law", but now live under "Grace" the new law of love. This also affected giving in the New Testament. The tithe remained the minimal standard of giving even though it is not referred to as often as it was in the Old Testament.

Influences of Jesus and the Apostle Paul on worship through giving in the New Testament are immense. Through their teachings a new attitude and thought on giving and the offertory evolve. Giving is still an act of worship to God, but emphasize a focus of generosity and missional works.

Jesus taught and talked about money and possessions throughout his ministry on earth. He recognized the temptations of both money and possessions, so he dedicated the majority of his parables to those topics. Christ spoke on the topic of money and possessions more than he spoke about salvation or other subjects in the Bible because he knew the lure and excitement of money would be great for many. Salvation calls us to turn away from sin, and the Bible gives specific guidelines on what constitutes sin. However, the Bible shares with us what can happen if we become obsessed with money or put wealth before the Lord. Jesus knew obsession with material possessions would severely challenge giving as an act of worship and limit our ability to following Jesus as disciples. As he stated in Matthew 6:21, " . . . for where your treasure is so will your heart will be also." Jesus warned believers that becoming attached to their money and possessions would cause a barrier to giving as an act of worship. "For the love of money is a root of all kinds of evil, and in their eagerness to be rich some have wandered away from the faith and pierced themselves with many pains" (1 Timothy 6:10).

The story of the widow's mite found in Mark 12:41-44 shares the attitude Jesus, and later Paul, promoted. Many of us who are familiar with the story fall short on understanding the woman's celebration, in giving an offering. Here is a widow who was her sole supporter and who struggled to support herself with basic necessities. Widows during biblical times were often the recipients of assistance. This widow loved the Lord and was proud of her faith. Though she was of very limited means she gives her last two mites as an offering unto the Lord. Others have more to give than the widow, but fail to discover her joy in giving. Their gifts were mere tokens, but the widow gave from the heart with a spirit of celebration.

Jesus makes it clear the offering was more than just giving or a payment of the Temple tax—it is an act of worship. In Matthew 5:23-24 Jesus said, "When you are offering your gift at the altar, if you remember your brother or sister has something against you, leave your gift there before the altar and go: first be reconciled to your brother or sister, and they come and offer your gift." Without question, this demonstrates that an attitude of harmony and reconciliation is vital for worship through giving.

The book of Acts depicts the early church in many scenes of generosity and unity. In Acts 2:43:47, the members made sacrificial offerings so the entire body of believers would have plenty. Verses 46-47 says, " . . . they ate their food with glad and generous hearts, praising God and having the goodwill of all the people." They gave to honor the Lord and celebrate their newly found salvation in Christ Jesus.

Apostle Paul, the great spiritual leader in the New Testament, taught why, when, where, and how believers should give an offering to the Lord. He gives clear instructions on giving in his letters to the church in Corinth. More importantly, Paul emphasizes the attitude with which a tithe or an offering should be presented. Through his teachings, he encourages us to be "cheerful givers" as we honor and worship the Lord through the act of giving.

In 1 Corinthians 16:2, Paul encourages the church in Corinth to follow the instructions he had given to the churches in Galatia. His instructions were detailed. An offering should be given on the first day of every week, indicating that giving is an act of worship that should take place regularly and systematically. This particular offering consisted of additional gifts that provided support for the church in Jerusalem.

Paul's second letter to the church in Corinth provides a foundation for the attitude in which believers should give. In chapters eight and nine, Paul continues to challenge believers to become generous in giving their offerings, primarily missional gifts. He mentions the attitude of the givers, particularly those in churches with limited means. Many of their members came from a lower socio-economic group but found joy in presenting an offering. The Corinthians, however, were residents of a major shipping center, filled with affluence, but they had not developed a spirit of generosity for others.

The churches of Macedonia may have been of limited means, but they possessed a wealth of generosity. In fact, in 2 Corinthians 8:4-6 Paul declares, " . . . begging us earnestly for the privilege of sharing in this ministry to the saints." Their contributions were a sign of celebration and generosity in supporting the Lord's work.

In 2 Corinthians 9, Paul writes to the church at Corinth to encourage them to provide missional support to the people of Macedonia. His letter was a letter of encouragement; it was an opportunity to teach these believers about giving, especially about the attitude with which the offerings are given. For many, the challenge was not one of scarcity, but one of willingness and joy in giving.

Paul teaches these believers that they are blessed to be a blessing to others in the gifts they present. But more importantly, the spirit in which the gift is given is just as important as the amount given. God calls believers who honor God with tithes and offerings to give out of their love for God, humanity, and the Lord's kingdom-building works. Verse seven describes the attitude in which to give an offering: "Each of you must give as you have made up your mind, not reluctantly or under compulsion, for God loves a cheerful giver."

With the church in Philippi, Paul again experiences the spirit of generosity. In Philippians 4:15-17, Paul expresses heart-felt gratitude for the support they graciously extended to his ministry when others did not. The members of the church at Philippi were of limited resources, much like the Macedonian churches. Paul praised them for their faithfulness in support of the ministry.

Giving to the saints was about celebrating God's generosity while providing resources for those in need. Through his teachings Paul wanted the affluent to find joy in giving locally and abroad.

The story of Anaisis and Sapphira in Acts 5 is arguably the most avoided story in the New Testament, as it relates to giving unto the Lord. Many people avoid the story because it is a biblical story that is at the core of faith and money. Pastors and laity seldom use this story as a scripture reference because it sparks of truth-telling and personal accountability. The consequences of Ananias and Sapphira's lie seem harsh and caused great fear among believers.

This story takes place in the early church when believers sold property and possessions, and shared everything in common. Ananias and Sapphira reneged on their promise to God to give the proceeds from the sale of a parcel of land to God's work. Instead, they only surrendered a portion of the proceeds for the Lord's kingdom-building work. Their desire to hold back some of the proceeds from the Lord's kingdom greatly disturbed Peter, but the fact that the couple lied to God distressed Peter even more. Further, they both had opportunities to make confessions to Peter, but refused to claim responsibility. The story of Ananias and Sapphira is a rich story because it deals with issues we struggle with today, like accountability. The lie they told was unnecessary, they felt they could lie to God, and felt they would not be held accountable to God or anyone else. Their lie and character flaw resulted in their sudden death.

We develop and cultivate giving to the Lord through spiritual growth and our personal relationship with the Lord. In the New Testament, we live under "Grace," but are called to be of a generous spirit. Our generosity is a reflection of God's generosity. Ananias and Sapphira did not understand the spirit of God's generosity, which ultimately resulted in their lack of trust in God. Lack of trust and faith, combined with their sin of lying, to the Lord caused their downfall.

In 2 Corinthians 9:7-8, Paul shared an excellent response to the story of Ananais and Sapphira as it relates to giving an offering: "Each of you must give as you have made up your mind, not reluctantly or under compulsion, for God loves a cheerful giver. And God is able to provide you with every blessing in abundance, so that by always having enough of everything, you may share abundantly in every good work."

God calls us to be cheerful givers as we continue to live under grace. The tithe still remains as the biblical standard for believers. Grace causes us to give beyond the tithe. Living under grace in the New Testament has transformed the heart and attitude of the giver toward worship through giving. It is because of God's unmerited gift of grace that we celebrate the offering.

O Gracious and loving God,
Allow us to be the generous givers you have
called us to be.
May we give out of our poverty,
as well as our affluence;
Let our gifts support mission and ministry near and far.
Bless our gifts so that lives will be touched and commu-
nities transformed.
In Christ name we pray. Amen.

CHAPTER THREE

Setting the Tone for Celebrating the Offering

Make a joyful noise to the Lord, all the
earth. Worship the Lord with gladness;
come into his presence with singing

PSALM 100:1-2

A pastor or minister serves as an example of stewardship in the life of the community of faith. Clergy have
a calling as Christ's disciples to live out and proclaim
the meaning of following Jesus. Sometimes that principle is already established, while in other congregations
it is developing. The process may be slow and purpose-
ful, or it may be quickly acclimated. Even though the
believer may not have a heart liberated to giving, it is
the goal to achieve a heart that is generous.

From the statement "ministry costs" to "the Lord loves a cheerful giver", the stage for celebrating the offering finds the worshiper in various places intellectually, spiritually and practically. Ministry is transformational even as it is also a budgetary item. What we offer to God as an act of ministry requires of our time, prayers, and gifts. As David proclaimed, "I will not offer to the Lord that which cost me nothing."

The role of the pastor is quite important in celebrating the offering. It is the pastor as spiritual leader and teacher along with the laity that helps define the ethos of money within a community of faith. As partners in ministry, pastors and clergy themselves may need to reorient their thinking and recognize that offerings are for more than something necessary to pay the bills.

Jesus clearly stated that "where your treasure is, there will your heart be also." So Sunday after Sunday, week after week, year in and year out, through sermons, teaching, conversation, and personal witness, believers can demonstrate their acts of worship and faithfulness.

As with any celebration, festive commemoration, or party, we know that celebrating lightens the burden and lifts up the heart of those participating. The individual who actively participate take the focus off of themselves and allow the moment to impact them. That's the real aim in celebration.

When Jesus mentioned the poor widow woman

who gave two copper coins and called his disciples to take heed to her gift, Jesus was showing us that this widow was giving out of her own need to worship. This poor woman was actively participating and taking the focus off of herself, what she had, or the lack thereof. She actively shared as a commemoration—a celebration that the life was a gift worth sharing.

When we deny the worshipper the opportunity to share in the life-giving experience of offering gifts to God, we deprived them from experiencing one of the joys of living. Here are some facets of Christian discipleship that connect with giving.

Spiritual Growth

Celebrating the offering is a spiritual discipline. Offering is as much a faith issue as our prayer life and worship. It is a lifeline to a relationship with the One who offers us life and to have it abundantly. While cultural standards say the accumulation of wealth and possessions constitute success, Christian discipleship requires looking at our offering as a discipline to develop our faith and trust in God.

In Matthew chapter 19, when Jesus challenged the rich young ruler to sell his possessions and give the proceeds away, he walked away disappointed, recognizing all that he would have to forfeit. As an act of love Christ gave his life for us and that is a sacrificial gift. Our offering is one expression of our gratitude to God. Just as exercise strengthens the athlete, spiritual discipline strengthens the believer.

Hands-On and Practical Experience

Our daily and personal experiences define who we are. Our life experiences nurture who we are and how we live out our purpose. Our life experiences also proclaim through witness and service our faithfulness to God. Poor decisions can hinder us to live out our dreams and God's vision. However, good experiences shape us also.

Those who receive gifts know how elated it is to be a recipient—the air of surprise, the anticipation of opening the gift and the resolve of its contents. Who does not like receiving a gift?

There is one area that we do not discuss often and that is gift giving. To offer a gift is an exciting experience also. Trying to consider a gift of value and significance, the joy of sharing the gift with the recipient, and finally to watch the response of the individual as the open the gift are fulfilling experiences.

So our everyday experience of giving and receiving is taken into the celebration of the offering. We try to create those memorable occasions for the member or worshiper, recalling the joy of gift giving and opening of a gift as the goal for the moment in worship.

Mental Growth

What am I doing? Why am I doing this? What will I get in return for doing this? The mind takes us through many obstacle courses and exercises.

Many worshipers and believers have heard sermons or Bible studies on the tithe, the one leper who came back to give thanks to Jesus for his healing, or Melchizedek. We know the story of Cain and Abel and their offering to God, etc.

When the heart and mind comes together, the believer will relish the thought that whatever state I find myself in I am content. God will supply for every need of ours according to God's riches in glory in Christ Jesus (Philippians 4:19). Remember all the words of the psalmist:

I was once young and now I'm old and I have never seen the righteous forsaken nor its seed begging for bread (Psalm 37:25).

Intentional Growth

The offering is an intentional activity. The offering is an act of worship that must be holistic. It meets believers where they are and allows them by acts of faith, experience, and intellect to participate in a planned part of worship.

Your place of worship, the atmosphere of the community of faith, the ethos of money, the view of ministry, and the understanding of scripture reflects how heightened the celebration will be. The planning and carrying out of the offering can make for an awesome transition and transformation for the worshipper.

L: When I was a child, I spoke like a child.

R: **Children are a blessing, a gift from God.**

L: We take pleasure in the children of church and neighbor,

R: **And we long to see what they will become as adults.**

L: When I became an adult,

R: **I grew beyond some parts of childhood.**

L: I grew in love; I grew in grace;

R: **I learned more of faith, hope, and love.**

L: As children and adults blessed by God, let us celebrate God's gifts with our offerings.

(Based on 1 Corinthians 13:11)

CHAPTER FOUR

The Offering Today

. . . remembering the words of the Lord
Jesus, for he himself said, "It is more
blessed to give than to receive."

ACTS 20:35

Giving is an act of worship. The offering is truly a time where all believers can actively participate in the worship service. In many of our congregations, the pastor stands before the congregation, announces it is time for the offering, and asks the ushers to please come forward. The ushers proceed to the chancel rail to receive the offering plates as if they work for Brinks or another security firm. Then, the offering is received, a prayer or doxology is given, and the offering segment of the service is finished. For many churches the offering feels like a brief interruption in the order of service. Instead, worship through giving is a time to inform and educate the congregation on life transforming ministries of the church, as well as biblical teachings. Moreover, it is a time to celebrate and honor God.

Churches and pastors who follow the lectionary can celebrate the offering even when the weekly lectionary text does not directly relate to financial gifts. Many of the lectionary texts center on some form of stewardship, which relates to an offering. The text may avail itself more to prayer, presence or service, but all are required to be good stewards. Still there is an opportunity to integrate giving in the offertory prayer using the lectionary text. Do not allow the lectionary to become a barrier, but let it inspire creativity in planning the offertory. Throughout this book you will find examples of litanies and other prayers based on scripture.

In the contemporary context of worship it is feasible for the worship leader to share with the congregation words and sentiments to encourage their praise and worship to go along with their celebration of the offering. It is of vital importance that you and I see "our all" is an offering "holy and acceptable unto God." Therefore, the offering should not appear to be an afterthought, but an intentional decision about celebrating the offering within the context of praise and worship.

Many members today pay monthly bills and other financial obligations electronically. Churches also have given their members the option of giving electronically. People who give electronically typically do not have anything to place in the offering plate. Provide them with a card or stamp to place on an envelope, so they can symbolically give in worship along with the rest of the congregation.[1] Further, encourage all members to place a five or ten dollar bill in the offering plate on the Sundays they are not giving electronically. This gives excellent witness and example to children and youth on giving as an act of worship, as well as helping develop the next generation of generous givers.

The offering is still an awesome act of worship unto the Lord. The presentation of God's tithes and offerings should be a time of great celebration. Giving in response to God's grace is cause for all Christians to give enthusiastically and cheerfully.

In this chapter, ideas and suggestions are made to enliven the offering celebration. Many of these ideas are simple, yet very powerful when shared with sincere belief and conviction.

CALL TO WORSHIP AND LITANIES

The call to worship is one of the most important parts of a worship service; it is the point in the service where all believers in the service are called to set their hearts, minds, and souls in a mode for worshipping and praising the Lord. In most congregations the pastor makes a powerful declaration for the call to worship. This establishes the tone for the entire worship service.

Consider offering a call to worship which centers on being stewards. This statement would remind members that we are stewards as well as worshippers. Stewardship of prayers, presence, gifts and service, may be integrated into the call to worship.

Create scriptural litanies that focus on our call to be stewards and our response to God. Adapt psalms and other passages of scripture into litanies. A call to worship or a litany with a stewardship theme given monthly will help create an atmosphere where a spirit of generosity will develop and grow.

Both the call to worship and litanies have the potential to set the tone early in the worship service for later in the service when the congregation hears the offertory. Express the call to worship with great conviction as you declare the significance of worship, and the importance of being a steward. Through the response of the litany, members will grasp a deeper spiritual understanding of being a steward and how to respond to God's grace.

THE INVITATION

Prior to the offering, the pastor or liturgist invites worshippers to participate actively in the offertory. The presentation of tithes and offering is significant part of worship because it is a tangible way in which all members can actively participate in worship through giving. Whether you are sitting in the pew, ushering, singing in the choir, an acolyte, liturgist, or a musician, you can participate by giving an offering. The invitation requires the worship leader to make a statement to the congregation to transition them into worship through giving. An invitation is a declaration or a biblically based statement that inspires and encourages believers to prepare for the presentation of their tithes and offerings.

A powerful, spiritual-filled invitation delivered with conviction and sincerity will enthuse members to give generously. Here are two examples of invitations to the offering:

1. "The Apostle Paul praised the Macedonian Christians for their giving. Now we are invited to give out of abundant joy, overflowing in a wealth of generosity."

2. "People of God, we have come praising God with song and spirit, now we come to praise with gifts and generosity."[2]

Invitations can be designed to center around seasons in the Christian year. Further, the same invitation may be used repeatedly as a mantra for a congregation.

READING SCRIPTURE

Scripture undergirds and grounds the Christian faith. Throughout the Bible, Christians discover verses and passages of scripture on the giving of tithes and offerings. Consider sharing scripture before the offering to present biblical insights into the presentation of our tithes and offerings.

Selected scripture readings do not have to be long, but must allow the hearers to receive the spiritual essence of the passage. It is imperative for the liturgists to read the scripture with conviction and enthusiasm. Read from a version that is easy to understand and comprehend. Further, adding a phrase at the end of the reading such as, "Let us celebrate in our giving," or "Be a cheerful a giver," can bring a sense of encouragement as well as enthusiasm to the entire congregation.

Sharing scripture always reemphasizes why,

when, where, how, and how much we should give. The Bible is the cornerstone of our faith and we must enlighten believers on what God requires of us. If money and possessions were not important, I do not believe Jesus would have spent so much of his time teaching and sharing parables on this subject. Apostle Paul probably would not have had so much to say concerning offerings that supported missional works in the New Testament, if believers possessed a spirit of generosity.

OFFERING MEDITATIONS AND REFLECTIONS

Once or twice monthly, share a brief offering meditation or reflection before lifting the offering. Offering meditations and reflections are brief, usually scripturally based one to two minute statements that offer practical insight into the presentation of our tithes and offerings. Reading meditations before the offering creates an atmosphere for celebrating the offering. "These meditations . . . create a biblical and theological framework for giving."[3] Further, these readings educate listeners on why, how, when, and the amount we should give to honor the Lord

In addition to inspiring words for giving, these meditations and reflections also offer insightful ways to look at our relationship in Christ and with others. Often listeners discover new ways of seeing how their gifts honor God and transform our lives as well as others. Other meditations address matters that focus on money and possessions and how they affect our relationship with the Lord, others, and our faith journey.

Creating offering meditations can be simple. Start with a biblical text or principle to develop a theme for the meditation. Give the theme a personal perspective, along with a life application. A good meditation can be as little as six to eight sentences. There are a number of excellent offering meditations resources available in Christian bookstores.

Reading offering meditations with conviction and sincerity will open generous hearts. These readings inspire, motivate, and educate listeners as they prepare to participate in worship through giving.

STEWARDSHIP STATEMENT

Many churches have mission and vision statements. These statements are posted in various areas of the church, located in the Sunday bulletin, placed in new members' guides, in newsletters, and on church web sites. Mission and vision statements reinforce what members believe as a congregation. Consider developing a stewardship statement for your church.

Once the statement is developed and approved by

the appropriate body of the church, designate a specific Sunday each month where the members say the stewardship statement in unison prior to receiving the offering. A stewardship statement articulates what the church and its members believe as stewards, and places the church membership in one accord. When shared with enthusiasm, it creates an ambience for celebrating the offering.

MINISTRY MOMENTS

Once a month prior to the offering, invite a member or members of an active ministry that transforms lives to share stories on how they are touching lives inside and outside the congregation. Ministry moments from ministry volunteers demonstrate how faith, ministry, and our tithes and offerings are linked together for the good of God's kingdom building works. Consider having a Scout leader or a troop member share his or her experience of being a part of the church sponsored troop, or a person who distributes clothes or food. Allowing people who serve in these ministries an opportunity to express their joy in serving in life transforming ministries to others in the congregation can create an atmosphere where congregants become eager to serve and support ministry. Members of the church are usually enthused by fellow members sharing how a ministry has made a difference in their lives as well as in the lives of those individuals whom they have touched.

Ministry moments allow believers to hear stories of kingdom building returns on their spiritual investments in the ministry of their church. These stories will inspire persons to give more faithfully to the ministry because they realize their tithes and offerings are doing more than paying for salaries, utilities, and maintenance. Their tithes and offerings are transforming lives and making a difference in the world.

The ministry moment should not be long. Three to five minutes or less will suffice. Talk about how the ministry involvement changed you, and how the ministry touched another person's life. Share a story of a child in Sunday school class, a child in the after school program who drew a picture of how the church placed a smile on his or her face, or how a person said, "Thanks for caring." These ministry moments can come from the church's involvement in building a "Habitat for Humanity" home, the senior's program, the adult enrichment classes offered to the community, and other life changing ministries of the congregation.

If your church has multi-media capabilities, share video clips of the featured ministry of the month while the ministry volunteer talks about his or her experience. If a video is not available, then a poster or an object that represents the ministry would help share the ministry.

Simply sharing from the heart is all that is needed to reveal the importance of a life-transforming ministry. Members are always excited to hear stories or see video clips on how their congregation is a ministry in action and responds to the needs of its members, the area in which the church resides, and the broader community.

GIVING TESTIMONIES

Giving testimonies has almost disappeared in our worship services. For many congregations it belongs in of the past. When society feels money and possessions are non-spiritual, there is a decline giving testimonies. People often take pride in the things they are able to accumulate, thus making giving testimonies countercultural. The truth of matter is that Jesus talked openly about money. Therefore, giving testimonies should be shared in worship on occasion.

Many members do not remember or have not witnessed a person sharing a giving testimony. But these testimonies are an important witness to God's generosity. Testimonies of the Lord's blessings and provisions are vital for a congregation of believers to hear.

Giving or stewardship testimonies are powerful in a number of ways. One of the best attributes of these testimonies is that they are usually given by laypersons. Laity can inspire and motivate other laypersons in ways clergy cannot. Clergy are expected to provide spiritual leadership in the area of giving, but a layperson is able to share a testimony without the risk of sounding self-serving. The person giving the testimony is the listener's "pew pal." The story of the person giving the testimony resonates with someone in the pew and becomes a voice of inspiration.

For two to three minutes before their peers, the members share a rehearsed testimony that communicates what motivates them to give. The testimony can be rehearsed before the pastor prior to the service or with someone who will provide honest feedback on the testimony. People must guard against sounding self-righteous, thus becoming a turn off. Further, they should also share when they discover the joy of giving and how giving became a part of their lives. A story on how giving affected their lives or their families' lives can help others see that giving is an act of worship and a celebration of God's generosity.

Giving testimonies may be shared with the congregation in the form an interview. These interviews will be longer than a typical testimony. The interviewer or pastor can ask the person questions like:

- What motives you to give?

- Have you always been a generous giver?

- What is the most exciting gift you have given?

- Is there a verse or passage of scripture that has influenced your giving practice?

Interviews typically take away some the fear of speaking in public and create an intimate atmosphere for receiving the member's witness and response to God's generosity.

These questions and the response to these questions from well-respected believers and leaders in a church will have a profound impact on the entire membership, thus creating a culture of faithful givers.

SKITS AND DRAMAS

Biblically based or scripturally referenced skits and dramas used prior to the offering can provide a positive lasting spiritual experience for congregants. People in our pews witness God's word in different ways. Some people are verbal learners and others are visual. Skits and dramas accommodate both learning styles. Viewing characters' roles in a skit often resonates with a number of persons who take time for brief self-reflection. Skit and dramas provide members with opportunities to learn and grow in their giving.

Present skits or mini dramas once or twice a year. A well-designed and rehearsed skit can take as little as five to fifteen minutes. The designated stewardship emphasis month is a great time to share a skit or mini drama during a worship service. The skit can be simply done with as few as two or three participants, or it can even be a one-person skit. Costumes are often not as important as the words or actions of the characters. The focus is always the Word of God.

The theme is vitally important and must be transparent. Two great Bible stories come to mind on the subject of generosity: the story of the widow's mite and the woman and the alabaster jar. A narrator begins by saying, "Let's look at the story of the widow's Mite." Picture a scene where people walk to a table where the offering plate sits, with their purses, wallets, and pockets filled with five, ten, and twenty dollars bills. One man pauses and searches to find a five dollar bill in the midst of a large wad of cash, another pulls out a couple of ten dollars bills from his wallet that he can barely put in his back pocket, yet another pulls out a credit card, so he can receive airline miles and hotel rewards points for his gift. Lastly, a woman slowly approaches the offering plate, searching and searching in her purse for something to place into the offering plate. Finally, she places her two coins in the plate. A narrator closes by saying, "Did you notice how the others only thought about giving more, or gave as if the offering was a tip? But this widow searched and searched her heart and purse. She gave her best and her all."

Throughout the Bible there are many stories that symbolize generosity. You do not have to limit these skits and dramas to biblical stories. Skits that center on sharing and generosity also help us to see that we are called to make a difference in the lives of others.

VIDEO CLIPS AND POWERPOINT

Today, we live in technological age when video conferencing, video clips, and PowerPoint presentations are part of our lives, particularly if we are in the workforce, school. or attend workshops and conferences. The gen-x, gen-y or millennial generations grew up with much of this technology. The rest of us have been immersed into this age, voluntarily or involuntarily. PowerPoint is a very common media tool that many are exposed to at work. Many churches have integrated PowerPoint and video clips in worship.

Contemporary worship services have used video clips and PowerPoint in their services for years. In recent years, many of our traditional churches have installed screens for video, PowerPoint, and better viewing throughout through the sanctuary and over-flow areas. These measures were implemented to appeal and relate to a younger generation of worship-pers. Video clips and PowerPoint are used to make a message come alive, to witness, and to teach.

Some churches use clips of their ministries to show members how their church is transforming lives in their community and around the world. Others show interviews of people whom the ministry of the church touched. A narrated presentation can also provide members with information on how their tithes and offering are making an impact in God's kingdom building.

OFFERTORY PRAYER

Prayer is important in the life of believers. So prayer, in relation to the offering, is also important. It is a means of communicating to God. Before and/or after the receiving of the offering, a prayer must be given. It communicates our gratitude and love of God's grace, love, mercy, protection, provision, and also petitions for God's blessings upon those gifts.

Offertory prayers can be given by the pastor or the liturgist, or said in unison by the worshipping body of believers. Weekly offertory prayers are avail-able at the website of the General Board of

Discipleship (www.gbod.org/stewardship). Typically, after receiving the offering, a doxology is given.

MUSIC

Musical selections are a very important part of celebrating the offering. The music and the musical selection can set the mood for a powerful worship experience through giving. A well-chosen hymn or piece of music can quickly reconnect the offertory back to the rest of the service. Our hymnals are full of anthems, hymns, and gospel music that center on God's grace and generosity and how we respond to God's love, grace, and mercy.

Music and singing are crucial elements in worship. Use hymns and gospel selections that lift up giving and stewardship. The lyrics of hymns like "You Can't Beat God Giving", "The Lord Is Blessing Me Right Now", "He Has Done Great Things for Me", "Give of Your Best to the Master", "What Shall I Render" possess deep theological meaning, which helps us understand more about our faith and God's grace.[3] Other hymns like "Bless Thou the Gifts", "What Does the Lord Require", and "What Gift Can We Bring" also create a spirit and an atmosphere for worship through giving.

Consider, on occasion or every week, using a processional during the offertory. In the African

American tradition, this is called "Traveling Music." An upbeat spirited hymn or gospel selection will energize members as they present their tithes and offering. "If You Want to Be Blessed" by Shirley Caesar will reconnect the offertory in most any congregation.

Pastors, worship leaders, and music directors must work together to carefully choose music that not only compliments the offertory but also coincides with the Christian season of the year. Great music and singing will cause a celebration through giving.

SERMONETTES

Pastors preach one stewardship sermon a quarter. Consider giving one or two brief stewardship messages or sermonettes every three months. These brief messages should be no more than five or six minutes in length. They are designed to educate and motivate members to see giving as a way of worshipping God. Also, they help members to see the connection between faith and money.

Sharing sermonettes should be brief and concise, highlighting a point with an illustration members easily relate to. These messages have the potential to transform the culture of giving in a congregation into one of generosity.

One cannot underestimate the power of these

brief messages. When shared with strong conviction and life application, hearts are changed. Changed hearts allow celebration through giving to take place.

DOXOLOGY

A doxology is a declaration of praise for all God has created, in heaven and on earth. It also acknowledges God's sovereignty and generosity, and creates the order of giving thanks. In our worship services a doxology given in response to the receiving of the offering allows us to praise and honor the Lord for all God does for us. Like many things in life, when we do them repetitively they sometimes lose meaning or power. Our doxologies have almost become a meaningless response given after the offering. Doxologies are much more than meaningless responses; they are cheerful and joyous responses to God's generosity.

Occasionally, prior to the receiving of the offering, explain the reason why we have a doxology. Read the words in the doxology and share their meaning. Insert a brief paragraph in the bulletin defining and explaining the meaning and reason for the doxology. Many members do not truly understand the words they sing each week in response to the receiving of the tithes and offerings.

"All things come of thee, O Lord; and of thine own have we given thee," is a doxology that is sung in many congregations across numerous denominations. There are some who do not know that it originates from 1 Chronicles 29:14b. In this pericope, King David is preparing to raise resources for the building of the temple. He recognizes that God has chosen his son Solomon (who is young and inexperienced) to build the temple, so he challenges his leaders and officers to make a freewill offering. They did so willingly and generously, just as he did. Then, David blesses God for God's greatness, power, glory, majesty, and generosity by saying, "All things come of thee, O Lord; and of thine own have we given thee."

The doxology "Praise God, from Whom All Blessings Flow" is awesome because it says with great conviction the acknowledgement from which all that we possess comes from. It honors the Lord who created us, and the provider of all things. The words in each of these doxologies center on recognizing, thanking, and praising the Lord for God's blessings and provisions. Those words should cause us to celebrate the worship act of giving.

BENEDICTION/SENDING FORTH

All worship services come to an end with a benediction, blessing, or a sending forth. As the congregation is sent out into the world, why not a offer parting word to encourage stewardship throughout the week?[4] This reemphasizes that we are called to be stewards of all resources the Lord has entrusted to us, with the closing words of the worship experience.

There are several ways to celebrate the offering in a worship service. To cause a celebration there must be intentionality and the presence of the Lord's spirit. With the offertory, planning is important, the spirit of the Lord must preside, and the Word expressed in gratitude. All of this must be undergirded in prayer. These are essential elements to authentic worship through giving.

Celebrating the offering means to worship the Lord with gladness as we come into God's gates with thanksgiving in our hearts. The Bible tells us we should not come empty handed. Our celebration displays our gratitude for God's generosity, protection, and provision. Truly, that is something all believers should enthusiastically celebrate.[5]

Gracious and merciful God,
we praise you as do the angels
And all the heavenly host.
We praise you as even all the
Creation offers praise.
In response to the call of Christ, we
Give our lives to you.

Even in this moment we celebrate the
Love of Christ for us and
for the world and we give these
Offerings for the sake of
Christ's work in the world. Amen.

END NOTES

1. Almetha Thomas, "E-Giving: Has Is Time Come for the Church?" (African-American Pulpit Digest, Summer 2002, Judson Press, Valley Forge, PA) p. 37

2. "How Important is the Sunday Morning Offering?" (United Church of Christ), 53.

3 Melvin Amerson, *Stewardship in African American Churches: A New Paradigm* (Nashville: Discipleship Resources, 2006), 75.

4. Wayne C. Barrett, *Get Well! Stay Well!* (Nashville: Discipleship Resources, 1997) 65.

5. Melvin Amerson, *Stewardship in African American Churches: A New Paradigm* (Nashville: Discipleship Resources, 2006), 78.

CHAPTER FIVE

Clergy's Role in Celebrating the Offering

"For God did not give us a spirit of cowardice, but rather a spirit of power and of love and of self-discipline."

2 TIMOTHY 1:7

The role a clergyperson in any congregation, large or small, rural or urban, is to be the spiritual leader of the congregation. Clergy are called to be spiritual leaders of all facets of the life of the congregation. Clergy are leaders in Bible study, administrative meetings, missional outreach, as well as in weekly worship, and in stewardship. In all areas in the life of a congregation, the pastor is the spiritual leader. Serving in the role of pastor, leadership requires one to be sincere and intentional in celebrating the offering.

PASTOR AS SPIRITUAL LEADER

Being the spiritual leader of a congregation requires pastors to perform duties as an administrator, servant, teacher and preacher. On occasion, this requires us to discuss and participate in matters that may make us feel uncomfortable. However, our calling is to follow Christ and sometimes we go into dangerous territory. Our discomfort does not allow us to ignore or arbitrarily delegate challenging tasks to other clergy staff or laity. For some, the offertory is a time when there is uneasiness or a loss of words or ideas. But the offering still must be lifted up in celebration.

In some congregations, pastors do no customarily talk or preaching on financial stewardship because the leaders in the church deem the topic non-spiritual. As pastors and spiritual leaders we must shed light on the 2,000 plus verses that center on money and possession, along with the parables Jesus taught. Recognizing the frequency of Jesus' discussions on the topic of money and possessions gives us a clue to the challenges that believers have gone through since biblical times on that vary subject. Don't hide! Proclaim the fullness of God's Word! Allow the Word to provide you with a source of strength and protection as you proclaim the Word of God.

In my work as a consultant to pastors, many become defensive and indicate they preach on all areas of stewardship: prayers, presence, gifts and service. Often, this is a strong indication that they camouflage the four areas by rolling them into one sermon, hoping not to upset members while attempting to encourage members to increase their financial support to the church. Give each area of stewardship its own message or sermon series before the congregation. Each area is a vitally important part of discipleship. Get over the fear and help the congregation grow in generosity, while celebrating the offertory.

Do You Practice What You Preach, or Preach What You Practice?

Once, I heard a preacher ask a question, "Do you preach what you practice?" or "Do you practice what you preach?" In other words are you setting a good example for the members of your congregation? Pastors are called to model or set an example for the entire congregation. Without question, pastors are also responsible for providing spiritual leadership as it relates to worship through giving. Its part of the calling!

God requires all believers to give the biblical minimum of a tithe. A tithe equates to ten percent of ones gross income. Often when it comes to tithing, people debate whether we should tithe on our gross or net income. The question becomes, "Would you rather be blessed on your gross or net?" Today with the various payroll deductions beyond taxes such as, savings, 401k, 403b, mortgage, car note, insurance premiums, "the net", has a new definition. For some it is basically whatever is left over. The original net income is based on after taxes. Again, we are to tithe as the biblical minimum standard. Mature givers do not get caught up in technical debates like gross or net, or argue if we have to tithe since we live under "grace." Believers who give from the heart usually give generously, and that measure often exceeds a tithe.

Like it or not, members observe their pastor because he or she is their spiritual leader and role model. Pastors must be tithers and generous givers in order to set good examples of steward. Recent seminary graduates, often saddled with immense student loan obligations, must make sincere earnest efforts in giving if they desire to lead the congregation in this area. Apostle Paul said in 1 Corinthians 4:2, "It is required of stewards to be faithful or trustworthy."

PRESENTING A WEEKLY OFFERING

Leaders Lead! As spiritual leaders and pastors, place an offering in the offering plate or basket each week. Members observe their pastor(s)' giving habits from the pews. They need to see their pastor participate in worship through giving as much as they see their pastor(s) in other areas of Christian discipleship. Further, clergy are not exempt from the practices they expect of the laity.

The issue of how often or when pastors get paid by their congregation determines the frequency of placing their tithes and offerings. Understandably, some receive their compensation monthly, bi-weekly, or weekly, but pastors should place a gift in the offertory plate weekly. Your major gift or full-tithe may be given on first Sunday or first and third Sunday, but an offering should be given on the rest of the Sundays of the month. Active participation in this portion of the service is as important as closing our eyes and bowing our heads for prayer, or singing a hymn. "On the first day of every week, each of you is to put aside and save whatever extra you earn . . . ." Paul shared that message with the church at Corinth, in 1 Corinthians 16:2. So, it is incumbent upon pastors to model their giving before the congregation weekly.

Many ministers will probably resent the question being told to make an offering each week. However, your congregants may not know what you give, but they can observe the frequency of your giving. Do not leave your giving or your lack of giving open for scrutiny or question. This is not an issue in most congregations, but it is an opportunity for pastors to set an example and standard before their congregations. Leaders lead!

BE . . .

The Bible tells us to be cheerful givers. On Sunday mornings or during your weekly worship service, pastors must not only be spiritual leaders, but cheerful givers. It is important that pastors demonstrate the joy of giving for their congregants.

In celebrating the offering it is crucial for pastors to be spiritual, unapologetic, intentional, and cheerful. All of these components are necessary for the offertory to become a celebration.

- Be *spiritual.* As pastor and spiritual leader it is important to convey messages the offertory is a spiritual matter, not a means of paying salaries and bills. Share with believers that our giving is a matter of the heart, faith, and our relationship with the Lord. Most importantly, use the Bible as your spiritual foundation.

- Be *unapologetic* while using the Bible to establish the spiritual foundation for giving as an act of worship. There are many Bible verses and stories to support your stewardship messages.

- Be *intentional.* There should be intentionality in the celebration of the offering. Plan your offertory time just as you would your weekly sermon. Prepare or choose an offering meditation or Bible verse for the worship time through giving.

- Be *cheerful.* Apostle Paul calls us to be cheerful givers. Your cheerfulness and enthusiasm is contagious and it will spread throughout the worship service and congregation. In fact, it will help cultivate a culture of generosity in a congregation.

The Spiritual Agitator

Many of you have heard of how pearls are formed. Pearls come from oysters. The oysters sift ocean water all day. Sand and minerals that are sifted agitate the oyster, causing a secretion that develops into a pearl. Pastors are spiritual agitators. Believers sift through God's Word, and many things in the Bible go against our culture, thus causing agitation. Through spiritual agitation, Christians grow. Help the spiritual pearl of generosity develop within members.

Partnering with Laity

Develop a working partnership with laity that celebrates the offering. Establish a worship committee if the church does not have one. When the worship service is planned, including the offertory, a spiritual synergy begins to take place. Pastors and laity need together to create powerful spiritual atmosphere for giving through worship.

Include laypersons in the offertory by using them as liturgist who read offering meditations. Allow laity to make giving testimonies, as well as share statements of support for special offerings. Worship is a shared experience for all believers, both clergy and laity.

Equipping laity to participate as liturgist or readers allows them to show their spiritual witness and encourage others to discover the joy of giving. Laity can influence other laity spiritually. Consider persons who generously support the ministry of the church, have a spirit of generosity, and have the E. F. Hutton appeal. ("When [they] talk, people listen.")

It's Worship!

The presentation of our tithes and offering is worship. It is worship through giving. The Bible tells us to "Worship the Lord with gladness" (Psalm 100:2). That includes the offertory! Our culture has made the discussion of money a taboo subject in the church. Without question, the offertory is a spiritual matter, no more private than praise and prayer. The negative stigma attached to money and giving to the Lord's work needs to come to an end. Jesus taught on money and possession often, because he knew money and material possessions have the potential to possess us, and serve as a god in our lives.

As worshippers we are to, "Enter his gates with thanksgiving, and his courts with praise" (Psalm 100:4). Worship through giving is included in this praise and thanksgiving.

It is the role of clergy to lead by example and teach congregants biblical principles of giving. In these teachings, pastors must be spiritual, unapologetic, intentional, and cheerful. With a partnership with laity, a transformation of the offertory into a celebration through giving will take place. Moreover, a culture of generosity will develop, whereby members talk openly and freely about supporting the ministries of the church.

L: The Bible invites us to be cheerful givers.

R: But we have bills to pay

L: And the money doesn't seem to go as far as it did.

R: God, are you teaching me a lesson in trust?

L: Am I walking with you, Lord Jesus?

R: In my grumbling a prayer of confession?

L: Am I moving to joy?

All: **Yes, I can praise your marvelous name, Lord! You have been present to me all the days past and all the days to come, and I will be of good cheer!**

CHAPTER SIX

Laity's Role in Celebrating the Offering

". . . and what you have heard from me
through many witness entrust
to faithful people who will be able
to teach others as well."

2 TIMOTHY 2:2

Weekend after weekend Christians fill sanctuaries and worship centers to worship and praise the Lord. Believers come to receive the Word and actively participate in the worship experience. Worshippers have immense roles in worship between the call to worship and benediction. Among congregants there are spiritual leaders who provide leadership in worship. Their role is to help create a positive, spirit-filled atmosphere for worship and praise. In fact, lay leaders influence others lay persons who sit in the pews. This includes the celebration of the offering. Leaders lead!

SPIRITUAL ROLE MODELS

Spiritual role models provide a great witness of generosity. It is not solely the responsibility of clergy to provide examples of stewardship or to communicate ways in which we celebrate the offering. Others in the congregation also reflect and reinforce the style of worship and praise of its leaders, both clergy and lay.

In congregations where a solid connection of faith and money have not been made, it is vitally important for laity in leadership roles to model giving as a spiritual response to God's grace. When believers view their leaders as being cheerful givers, then others will begin to embrace their spirit of celebrating the offering.

Money has become a topic that is often avoided in our society because it is deemed a private matter. In light of the way society views money, the church often reflects the same viewpoint. However, the Bible tells us in Romans 12:2, "Do not be conformed to this world, but be transformed by the renewing of your minds, so that you may discern what is the will of

God—what is good and acceptable and perfect." Leaders have an opportunity and an obligation to reverse this prevailing trend in our local congregations.

Fear Factor

Laity, like pastors, need to overcome the fear factors that are associated with the discussion of money in a congregation. Remember, money and possessions were discussed often throughout the Bible, so there must have been several good reasons for the redundancy on the topic. Jesus and Apostle Paul talked and taught on the subject of faith and money because they recognized how money and possession could possibly possess us. Apostle Paul, throughout his ministry, encouraged and challenged believers to experience giving as a joyful experience in which we connect with God and others. To overcome the fear factors connected to public discussions of money amongst peers in our congregation requires that one use the Bible as the primary reference, and help others to see the correlation between biblical texts and life application. The Bible is still a spiritual source for our faith. Use it to calm fears about the discussion of money and possessions.

Apostle Paul said, "God did not give us a spirit of cowardice" (2 Timothy 1:7). This should give us the courage to witness our spirit of generosity to others believers. It is important for laity to boldly express their faith through giving. Many believers seek the spiritual witness of other believers as they grow in Christian discipleship.

Partners in Worship

Laity are in partnership with the pastor or the pastoral staff of the congregation. All believers and members are partners in corporate worship, at each and every worship service. As partners in the body of Christ, and in corporate worship, we are called to witness our faith before God and one another. No one in worship has a monopoly on praise and worship. This includes celebrating the offering.

It is important for laity to worship through giving in the same spirit and enthusiasm as Christians displayed in 2 Corinthians 9:6. They gave cheerfully and they felt it was a privilege to give to the Lord's work, even though they were not wealthy. The members of the Macedonian church found great joy in giving.

In order for the offertory to become a time of celebration, a great level of sincerity and intentionality must be present. With intentionality comes a plan to create an atmosphere where people can experience a spirit of generosity. Lay participation is vital if a spirit of generosity is going to permeate throughout the congregation. Participation goes beyond placing offertory envelops in the offering plate. As mentioned in chapter four, it requires laypersons to read scripture, share an offering meditation before the offering, or give testimonies and statements of support.

Setting an Example

As spiritual role models, believers must be willing to set an example for others believers to follow. This necessitates one to be intentional in his or her worship through giving. It is important for leaders to place an offering into the offering plate each Sunday, even though they may give electronically or give the majority of their tithes and offerings one set Sunday. Leaders lead. New Christians or members, who may be less ground in the Word, observe and witness these actions as they relate to giving.

The offering on Sunday is a not private matter, because others can see your eagerness or lack of eagerness as the offertory plates are passed. Apostle Paul said in 2 Corinthians 8:12, "For if the eagerness is there, the gift is acceptable according to what one has—not according to what one does not have." The spirit and enthusiasm in which we give is important when we attempt to create an environment where the offering is considered a celebration through giving.

Ushers

Ushers in our churches provide a great service in worship services every Sunday. However, occasionally smiles are absent from ushers. Often an usher is the first person a visitor a member comes in contact with once inside the sanctuary. Ushers extend hospitality. A smile is important! It sets in motion a sense of kindness and warmth about a congregation.

Smiles are also contagious. In fact, Apostle Paul encourages us to be cheerful givers. A smile or a cheerful expression before and during the offertory helps set the tone for celebrating the offering. Members seeing an usher smile as they pass the offering plate will often reciprocate a smile as they place their gift into plate. This will create an atmosphere for celebration.

In partnership with the pastor, consider processing to the chancel rail to receive the offertory plates or baskets, without being asked verbally. A signal from the pastor or worship leader can initiate the procession, such as a nod, hand gesture, or an offering invitation statement. This will allow for a smooth transition to the celebration through giving.

Laity, in partnership with pastor, can positively and spiritually transform the worship experience of giving. It only takes intentionality, a spirit of generosity, a smile or a positive facial expression for the celebration through giving to begin. Remember, we are spiritual role models!

Bless, O Lord, these gifts that they may feed the hungry, clothe the naked, visit those in prison, elevate the downtrodden, heal the sick, and comfort those in need. Bless these gifts, Lord, that they may become your hands and heart in the world. Amen.

CHAPTER SEVEN

Children and Youth
Celebrating the Offering

Training children in the right way,
and when old, they will not stray

PROVERBS 22:6

Children and youth have a place in worship! They are equal partners in the body of Christ. In fact, Jesus felt they were so precious and important that he said, "Let the little children come to me, and do not stop them, for it is to such as these that the kingdom of heaven belongs" (Matthew 19:14). Somehow, children and youth are typically given little attention as it relates to worship through giving.

The reasons why little focus has been given to this group of worshippers range from, "they are only children" to "they don't have any money." Children and youth are still members of the body of Christ. Our children and youth are part of our church today, and they can lead us even more as they become the future spiritual leaders of tomorrow.

There must be intentionality in integrating our younger members in worship, as well as creating worship through giving in a way that they will understand giving as an act of worship. Create teachable moments to help young believers learn giving as a response to God's grace. These teachable moments may take place in the regular worship service, children's church, Sunday school, and youth fellowship. Adults, children, and youth must see you place more than a token dollar bill in the offertory plate weekly. Some of church members support the church by making electronic contributions or give on the first and fifteenth of the month. Consider placing something extra in the plate each week so they will understand the difference between a tithe or proportionate gift, and an offering, which is over and above our regular giving.

It is incumbent upon church leaders and parents to develop the next generation of generous supporters of the church. This chapter shares ideas to create an environment where both children and youth can actively participate in worship through giving.

WORSHIP

Worship is not exclusively for adults. Consider how children and youth can connect with the message while being in the presence of their parents and other elders. Special consideration should be given too for children who attend children's church without their parent(s) present. Developing a healthy attitude toward the offertory is helpful for children or youth to understand celebration of the offering. Helping young members to understand that all we have belongs to God is important. God's grace and our response is why we give to the Lord's work. Otherwise, our young will never connect faith and money, with worship.

Teachable moments are vital. Those moments can be provided in various setting in the life of the church. Depending on a church's style of worship, a children's message is always appropriate, during the worship service. A children's stewardship message has the potential to affect the entire congregation. By hearing the message together, the entire family has the opportunity to further discussion the topic of worship through giving. Further, parents and grandparents always pay close attention to what is being taught to their loved ones, so it becomes a teachable moment for the entire family. I would encourage a stewardship message for children and youth at least once a quarter, just as I would recommend a steward-ship sermon for the adults. The messages can be shared on the same day, using the same scriptural text, thus allowing the family to embrace the same message.

Allow young believers to participate in the lifting of the offering by reading offering meditations or scripture as members present their tithes and offerings. Preferably, this will take place on regular Sunday, as opposed to a Children's or Youth Sunday. Having a young people share in the reading of scripture or a meditation during worship not only reinforces they are participants in worship, but more importantly helps them connect faith and money while celebrating the offering. Also, their peers see their witness through these readings.

Churches that have separate children's or youth church must intentionally plan the celebration of the offering for their service. Having the same theme or message as the adult service develops continuity. Remember Proverbs 22:6, "Train children in the right way, and when old, they will not stray." Further, children of today have financial resources that past generations did not possess, thus making this an opportune time to teach biblical stewardship and celebration of the offering.

Children and youth have many lessons to teach us. Let them speak to the whole church through their own creative approaches to offerings and stewardship. Many of our children and youth are creative. Give them opportunities to utilize their creativity in worship. A brief, biblically based skit not only lets them share their talent, but also conveys a contemporary message of God's generosity and our call to respond to that generosity. The Message Bible, with it's contemporary language, is a helpful resource for youth creating skits. The skit should take less than ten minutes.

Challenge a child or a youth to write a poem as a response to a passage of scripture on generosity or a mission work experience, and ask him or her to share it during the offertory. Children or youth might also occasionally give a children's message during service.

SERVICE

In many congregations, youth groups participate in mission projects in their local communities as well as around the country and the world. The youth who work in these projects often go places where the people they are helping are financially, and educationally less fortunate than the youth group. Building shelter, clinic, and school facilities are often part of the mission trips. The mission trip itself has little directly to do with celebrating the offering, but it is very helpful in developing generosity. "Growing Up Generous" encourages churches to give young people opportunities to talk about and reflect on their financial giving.[1]

Gen-Xer's and Millcnials are typically service oriented. They enjoy hands-on ministry, and take great joy and pride in making a difference. These generations give time and money to projects or institutions they deem are transforming lives and quality of life. Max Mertz, Director of the Wesley Foundation at Texas A&M University, contends that Gen-Xer's and Millenials are motivated in their giving when they see real needs and are able to see tangible results. Further, he strongly feels mission projects motivate and inspire giving in groups. A strong, compelling vision of life changing, community transforming ministries really touches the hearts of this group of believers, which causes them to give.[2]

With characteristics of Gen-X and Millenials in mind, provide annual mission opportunities for them while allowing them to share their experience with the congregation. Their testimony will touch the life of other youth and adults. This experience connects grace, faith, works, and money, which leads to celebration through giving.

Today, many children and youth have their own money. They either have part-time jobs or receive an allowance from their parents. It is important for them to understand that everything belongs to God, and that they are to honor God with a tithe of all their allowance or earnings. Helping them to biblically understand they are to give, irrespective of their age, is vitally important in developing the next generation of generous givers. Instill the joy of giving through Sunday school, youth fellowship, and children's church.

Consider allowing these young believers to design their own offertory envelope. Develop an offering envelope for children and another for youth. Having their own envelop will allow them to grow in Christian discipleship and faith and help them to see that they are to honor God with their first fruits. Provide at least one or two additional giving opportunities on the offering envelopes in addition to a tithe or proportionate gift, such as funding for mission projects. This group of believers loves to support mission related projects. Further, these resources may be allocated or designated for their annual mission trip project. However, use caution when designated gifts exceed regular gifts.

Celebrating the offering is for all believers. It is important for church leaders to recognize giving paradigm shifts among children and youth of today. Each generation looks at church support differently, so presenting the biblical message, along missional works, touches the hearts of these young believers. Give them opportunities to share their stories of faith and works with the congregation, but also with their passion for transforming lives and communities. Knowing they are making a difference in the world motivates them to celebrate the offering and worship through giving.

L: God is good

R: All the time!

L: God gives life

R: All the time!

L: God loves us

R: All the time!

L: God is good

R: All the time!

END NOTES

1. Roehlkepartain, Eugene C., Elanah Dalyah Naftali and Laura Musegades, "Growing Up Generous: Engage Youth in Giving and Serving" (The Alban Institute, Bethesda, MD, 2000),107.

2. Mertz, Paul "Max", Director of the Wesley Foundation at Texas A&M University at College Station.

CONCLUSION

Celebrating the offering is a spiritual act of worship every believer can actively participate in each week. Giving becomes a celebration when the believer discovers the joy of generosity, which grows out of God's grace. This celebration is our regular response to God's generous gift of grace.

Unfortunately, for many individuals and congregations the joy and the spirit of generosity that comes out of the offertory celebration does not come naturally. Most Christians grow in generosity as they grow spiritually. Churches grow in generosity when stewardship is preached, taught, embraced, and celebrated.

In order for the celebration to occur, a process of transformation needs to take place. As a multi-generational society, the church has discovered how members from the various age groups view the church and money differently. Thus, the church must to be more intentional in nurturing generosity, particularly as it relates to the various groups that are represented in our local churches. Even in light of their varying views of the world, the Bible still stands as the standard and guide for all Christians. However, leaders my need to tailor or alter the method for sharing the message of God's generosity for the Silent generation, Boomers, Busters, Gen-Xer's, Millennials, and so on.

Pastors and laity must develop a plan that celebrates and openly discusses the offering. The tone for the offertory takes place before the invocation or the call to worship. It begins when the pastor and laity, in partnership, create a systematic approach that spiritually practically, and mentally touches members' hearts, minds, and souls throughout the year spiritually, while also being intentional in setting the tone for the celebration through giving.

This process will not just take place during Sunday worship and administrative committee meetings, but will eventually take place in all facets of church life, as the spiritual DNA of generosity of the church is transformed. With a year-round stewardship plan undergirded with prayer, sermons, Bible studies on stewardship, and an intentional integration of the offertory in the worship service, believers will begin to connect their faith and money. At that point true believers will be able to say with great conviction, "Let's celebrate the offering!"

Appendices

Celebrating the Offering Suggested Schedule

Weekly

- Offertory prayer
- The Invitation
- Doxology

Monthly

- Laity read offering meditation
- Stewardship Statement
- Stewardship focused scripture reading

Quarterly

- Litany/Call to Worship
- Stewardship Sermon
- Sermonette
- Ministry Moment or Ministry Video Clip/ PowerPoint

Annually
- Stewardship Sermon Series (Stewardship Month)
- Stewardship Skit

LITANIES AND CALLS TO WORSHIP

We Give Joyfully

(Based on Acts 3:1-8)

Leader: God does not ask for silver and gold.

Response: God asks for what we have.

Leader: We are asked to give joyfully and to share with others.

People: Silver and gold we do not have, but what we have we give joyfully today.

All: **Amen.**

Rev. Maxine Allen

It All Belongs to God

Leader: The earth is the Lord's and all that is in it

. . .

(Psalm 24:1)

Response: For it all belongs to God.

Leader: All tithes from the land . . . are the
Lord's they are holy to the Lord

(Leviticus 27:30)

Response: For it all belongs to God.

Leader: Bring the full tithe into the storehouse,
so that there may be food in my house.

(Malachi 3:10)

Response: For it all belongs to God.

Leader: Honor the Lord with your substance and
with the first fruits of all your produce.

(Proverbs 3:9)

Response: For it all belongs to God.

Leader: On the first day of every week, each of
you is to put aside and save whatever
extra you earn, so that collections need
not be taken when I come.

1 Corinthians 16:2

All: Let us honor the Lord with the presentation of
our tithes and offerings, for it all belongs to
God. Amen.

Rev. James Amerson

Honor the Lord

Leader: Make a joyful noise to the Lord, all the earth, Worship the Lord with gladness; come into his presence with singing.

(Psalm 100:1)

Response: I will honor you with praise, because you are my creator, sustainer, comforter and supplier of all my needs.

Leader: Where your treasure is, so will your heart be also.

(Matthew 6:21)

Response: My heart and my treasures belong to you O Lord.

Leader: Honor the Lord with your first fruits.

(Proverbs 3:9)

Response: I will not only honor you O Lord with my first fruits, but I will honor you with my whole life.

Leader: Remembering the words of Jesus, "It is more blessed to give than to receive."

(Acts 20:35)

All: In honoring the Lord, we praise, worship, serve, and give to whom all blessings flow. Let us give cheerfully with our whole heart, as Christ gave his all for us. Amen.

Rev. Melvin Amerson

A Litany of Generosity

All: Dear Lord,

We come before you today to ask you to help us be more generous. We pray:

Leader: Gracious God, Give us generous hearts . . .

All: . . . so we may fully appreciate all your many blessings to us.

Leader: Gracious Savior, gives us generous hearts . . .

All: . . . so we may generously give without counting the cost.

Leader: Gracious Redeemer, give us generous hearts . . .

All: . . . so we may share in love without expecting something in return.

Leader: Gracious Deliverer, give us generous hearts . . .

All: . . . so we may know the joy that comes from serving others.

Leader: Gracious Sustainer, give us generous hearts . . .

All: . . . so we may bless others as we are blessed by you.

Leader: Gracious King, give us generous hearts . . .

All:	. . . so we may hold all our treasures in an open hand of generosity.
Leader:	Gracious Giver, gives us generous hearts . . .
All:	. . . so we may recognize all your many blessings in each new day.
Leader:	Gracious Provider, give us generous hearts . . .
All:	. . . so we may learn the difference between what we need and what we want.
Leader:	Gracious Giver of life, give us generous hearts . . .
All:	. . . so we may ever thank you and serve you.
Leader:	Almighty God, we ask this, knowing that you will always give us all that we need, bless the work, we do for you today and always, in Jesus' Name. Amen.

Rev. Rose M. Booker-Jones

Everything

Leader:	Everything we have comes from God.
People:	We love, because God first loved us.
Leader:	Everything we have comes from God.
People:	We pray, because Jesus taught us to pray.

Leader: Everything we have comes from God.

People: We offer ourselves and our gifts, because Jesus died for us.

All: Everything we have comes from God. Through these gifts, we offer our hands and our hearts to God. May these gifts be used to further the ministries of our church and to offer Christ to all. Amen.

Chris Davis Garcia

We Are

Leader: We are children of God. Let us praise God this day and worship him with our prayers.

People: Our hearts are filled with love for Our Savior.

Leader: We are children of God. Let us praise God this day and worship him with our presence.

People: Our minds are centered on God's work for the kingdom.

Leader: We are children of God. Let us praise God this day and worship him with our gifts and our service.

People: Our hands are ready to serve others, and our gifts are offered with shouts of

thanksgiving for all that God has done
for us.

All: Praise God! Amen.

Chris Davis Garcia

Sharing Our Blessings

Leader: "Give liberally and be ungrudging when
you do so, for on this account the Lord
your God will bless you in all your work
and in all that you undertake."

Deuteronomy 15:10

Response: Lord, you have entrusted us with much.
May we appreciate what we have and be
challenged to share our blessings with
those less fortunate than ourselves.

Leader: "How does God's love abide in anyone
who has the world's goods and sees a
brother or sister in need and yet refuses
help? Little children, let us love, not in
word or speech, but in truth and action."

1 John 3:17-18

Response: We cannot attain true happiness through
the accumulation of possessions. We
must learn to give from the depths of
our heart as you have taught us to love
one another.

Leader: "Like good stewards of the manifold grace of God, serve one another with whatever gift each of you has received. Whoever speaks must do so as one speaking the very words of God; whoever serves much do so with strength that God supplies, so that God may be glorified in all things through Jesus Christ."

1 Peter 4:10-11

Response: Everything we have belongs to you, Lord. You have bestowed your grace freely on us providing us with all we have and all we are. You have given us the gift of life.

All: "Each one of you must give as you have made up your mind, not reluctantly or under compulsion, for God loves a cheerful giver. And God is able to provide you with every blessing in abundance, so that by always having enough of everything, you may share abundantly in every good work. Thanks be to God for his indescribable gift!"

2 Corinthians 9:7-8 and 15

Joyce Russell

A Litany on Stewardship

Let us pray:

Leader: Almighty and everlasting Father, we give thee thanks this day, for the fruits of the earth in due season and for the labors of those who harvest them.

Response: Lord, increase our resolve to share your blessings with others.

Leader: For out of your boundless reservoir of love, mercy, grace, and generosity, you continue to meet our every need.

Response: Lord, increase our resolve to pass on these unmerited gifts, so that others may come to know you as we so often claim that we do.

Leader: For we are indeed mindful of those who came before us, many who labored without any reward, but who cast their sometimes meager bread upon the waters of life, so that we may enjoy this abundance.

Response: Lord, lest we forget, increase our resolve to have enough compassion for the continuous funding of those bridge building opportunities that will enhance body, soul and minds of unborn generations.

Leader: O God, who has so greatly loved us and
           mercifully redeemed us, in spite of our
           sinful ways.

Response: Save us and help us to become more like
           you each and everyday.

Leader: Father, you who did not spare your only
           begotten son, but gave him up for us all,
           and who with him has freely given us all
           things.

All: Receive our offerings which we bring
           before you and dedicate to you this day.
           Enable us as we come with all our gifts
           and ourselves to thee, that with body,
           soul and spirit, we may truly serve and
           worship you, and, in our service to you
           find our deepest joy. Amen.

Rev. Homer D. Williams

OFFERTORY PRAYERS

Lord, I see your face in the homeless man. Lord, I
see your face in the child at play. Lord, I see your
face in those who are at the bus stop. May our
offering help this church to minister to all of God's
children. Amen.

Rev. Maxine Allen

As we write our checks and place our cash in the offering envelopes let our praise to you, oh, God be demonstrated. As our children place their coins in the plate our ushers and acolytes lift the offering to you: may our praise be demonstrated to you, oh God, Amen.

Rev. Maxine Allen

Bless Oh, Lord, gift and giver to your service. We give because we have received. You have given us life and salvation through Jesus Christ. We give in gratitude, expecting only that the gift of ourselves and our resources in your service will help redeem someone along the way by your grace. Amen.

Dr. L. James "Jim" Bankston

My heavenly Father,
Your word teaches me that you will make grace
    abound to me,
So that in all things, at all times, I will have all that
    I need.
You are present in every good work that I do,
Keep blessing my hands and my service to others.
Oh Lord, I know that you want me to share with
    others the love you demonstrate in my life,
You provide me with plenty so that I can give to
    others,
You have assured me that I cannot give too much
    because your grace is limitless.

I believe that my obedience demonstrates my love
for you.
O Lord, I pray that my stewardship is pleasing and
my efforts are blessed in the name of Jesus, I
pray, with much love and thanksgiving. Amen.

Sandra C. Cranford

(Based of Psalm 146. To read in unison.)

Happy are those whose help is the god of Jacob,
Whose hope is in the Lord,
Who made heaven and earth,
Who keeps faith forever!
Who executes justice for the oppressed;
Who gives food to the hungry;
Who sets the prisoners free;
Who opens the eyes of the blind;
Who lifts up those who are bowed down;
Who watches over the strangers and aliens;
Who upholds the orphan and the widow.
This is our God, and this is the God we greet with
our offerings.

Rev. George Donigian

Gracious God, as we prepare ourselves for the offering this day, keep us ever mindful that we are the
trustees of all you have given us. Remind us that it is
through you that we are so richly blessed with all that
we have our lives, our families and our possessions.

Let us meditate on how we have been blessed by your generosity. Oh Father, help us, as we return to you our tithes and offerings to you, for your work in this church and throughout the world, so that we may be a blessing to others. In Christ's name, we pray. Amen.

Ed Engleking

Accept this offering, O God, as a token of our earnest desire to be responsible stewards, an expression of our love for you, and a sign of our willingness to be of even greater service in the future; in Jesus' name. Amen.

Dr. James "Jim" F. Jackson, Jr.

Gracious and loving God, giver of life and source of strength, we know that all we have received is from you. You call us to be stewards of your abundance, the stewards of all you have entrusted to us. Teach us to always use your gifts wisely and to share them generously. Send the Holy Spirit to work through us, in us, and with us as we bring your message to those we serve. May our faithful stewardship testify of the love of Jesus Christ in our lives. In Jesus' name, we pray with generous hearts. Amen.

Rev. Rose M. Booker-Jones

Gracious God, we praise your Holy Name.
We thank you for your grace, mercy and love
toward us this day.

We come into your presence thanking you for
our life, talents and spiritual gifts freely given to us.
We ask that these gifts be used in the building and
maintaining your heavenly presence on earth.

Please accept our tithes, offering and sacrificial
gifts for your honor and glory.

This is our prayer and my petition in Jesus
Christ. Amen.

Rev. James A. Richie

Generous God,
We give you praise for your extravagant love. Touch
our hearts today and continue to create in us giving
spirits. Teach us to be just as excited about giving,
as we are about receiving. Give us a spirit of joy as
we share our tithes and offerings this. In the name
of Jesus, God's greatest gift to us all. Let the giving
people of God, say, **Amen.**

Rev. Renita Thomas

Eternal and holy God, this worship service and this
offering remind us that without You, known in
Jesus Christ, we are empty-handed. So make our
tithes and offerings praise to you and to be a blessing to others in telling the Good News of Jesus
Christ in our hometown and around the world. May
this time of worship and this moment of giving help
us to re-focus our lives to be the persons and the
families and the people you have called us to be as

faithful disciples of Jesus Christ. In whose mighty name and with a renewed commitment to his will we pray. Amen.

Rev. James Varner

Creator God,
We give thanks for all we have received. Thank you for the ability to recognize the lows so we can appreciate the highs. We recognize hunger so we may be thankful for the plentiful. We recognize sickness so we may be thankful for the healthy. We recognize the homeless so we may be thankful for homes and family. Help us to recognize all we have comes from you. Accept this offering as a token of our gratitude and understanding of both what you have given to us and our responsibility to help all of your children and our brothers and sisters in Christ. Give us the strength and understanding to use all the resources as you would have us to use them. In your son's names, Jesus Christ, the Savior, we pray. Amen.

Curtis Vick

Lord, give us what we need to live faithfully and serve you. Don't give us all that we desire, for we want far too much for our own good. You don't need to give us everything that our neighbors have, just give us what we need. We are bold to pray, give us this day our daily bread. Teach us to live a life of contentment, the joy of being satisfied with what we have and the freedom that comes from being released from striving. For all your good gifts, we give thanks, especially we thank you for the daily gifts of food, of family, and friends, those ordinary ways that you show your daily care for us.

Dick Young

(The following prayers were written by
Melvin and James Amerson.)

Parents often give increases in their children's allowance as they mature. Typically, there is an increase in responsibility with the increase. God does the same with adults. God increases our earnings and provisions so we are able to give more to disciples-building ministries. It is said in Luke 12:48, "To whom much is given, even much more will be required." Let us worship the Lord in our giving.

I heard a pastor once say, "You can't pay God back, but you can pay God forward." Consider giving as the Lord has blessed you. Joshua 24:15, says, ". . . for me and my household, we will serve the Lord." Part of serving the Lord is presenting God's tithes and our offerings unto God. Let us present our tithes and offerings from this day forward.

"Give and it will be given to you pressed down, shaken together, running over, will be put into your lap, for the measure you give will be the measure you get back" (Luke 6:38). This verse of scripture sounds like an investment plan. God's tithes and offerings are much like a mutual fund. When we give collectively as a body of believers that is what will occur in our congregation. The overflow of resources can be used to further transform lives and build the kingdom of God. Let us present our tithes and offering into God's mutual fund.

There was a time when sports agents would earn a fee of ten percent of an athlete's contract just for negotiating the contract. The agent would receive the entire amount off the top, regardless of what took place after the signing of that contract. For some reason, people resist giving a tithe or ten percent to God, who negotiates every turn and facet of our lives. Let us present our tithes in gratitude for what the Lord continuously does for us.

"For where your treasure is, there your heart will be also" (Matthew 6:21). This verse is so true, when we examine our checkbook or credit card statements. God calls us to be generous, as God has been generous to us. The things we treasure we tend to eagerly support. How does your support of the Lord's work measure compared to the other things you treasure? Let us give as God has generously given to us.

SUGGESTED RESOURCES

Amerson, Melvin, *Stewardship in African American Churches: A New Paradigm*, Discipleship Resources, Nashville, TN, 2006.

Bridgeman Davis, Valerie and Safiyah Fosua, *The Africana Worship Book*, Discipleship Resources, Nashville, TN, 2006.

Ball, Arthur E., *Let Us Give*, Kregel Publications, Grand Rapids, MI, 2003.

Bible, Leon, *Tithe and Offering Scriptures Volumes 1-4*, Ministry Helps, Lauren, SC, 2001.

Cloughen, Charles, Jr., *One Minute Stewardship Sermons*, Morehouse Publishing, Harrisburg, PA, 1997.

Cloughen, Charles, Jr., *Sixty-Second Stewardship Sermons*, The Liturgical Press, Collegeville, MN, 2000.

Carter, William G., *Speaking of Stewardship: Model Sermons on Money and Possessions*, Geneva Press, Louisville, KY, 1998.

Fuller, Elmer B., *Effective Meditations for the Offering and Communion*, iUniverse.com, Inc., Lincoln, NE, 2000.

Halverson, Delia, *Let The Children Give: Time, Talents, Love, and Money*, Discipleship Resources, Nashville, TN, 2007

Miles, Ray, *Offering Meditations*, Chalice Press, St. Louis, MO, 1997.

Moseley, Dan, *Joyful giving: Sermons on Stewardship*, Chalice Press, St. Louis, MO, 1997.

Mosser, David, and Brian Bauknight, *First Fruits: 14 Sermons on Stewardship*, Abingdon Press, Nashville, TN, 2003.

Roehlkepartain Eugene C., Elanah Dalyah Naftali, and Laura Musegades, *Growing Up Generous: Engaging Youth in Giving and Serving*, The Alban Institute, Bethesda, MD. 2000.

Walker, Roby, *Money Talks: Stewardship Devotions for Worship*, Pathway Press, Cleveland, TN, 2001.

Watley, William D., *Bring the Full Tithe: Sermon on the Grace of Giving*, Judson Press, Valley Forge, PA., 1995.